W9-AUK-775

SUPER BOWL SUPERSTARS

AARON RODGERS
and the
Green Bay Packers

SUPER BOWL XLV

by Michael Sandler

Consultant: James Alder
Football Expert
football.about.com

BEARPORT
PUBLISHING

New York, New York

Credits

Cover and Title Page, © AP Photo/Eric Gay; 4, © AP Photo/Kevin Terrell; 5, © AP Photo/Kevin Terrell; 6, © Bill Husa/Chico Enterprise-Record; 7, © Chico Enterprise-Record; 8, © Glenn Fuentes/Chico Enterprise-Record; 9, © Glenn Fuentes/Chico Enterprise-Record; 10, © Donald Miralle/Getty Images; 11, © Tom Berg/NFL/Getty Images; 12, © Jonathan Daniel/Getty Images; 13, © AP Photo/ Morry Gash; 14, © Bill Frakes/Sports Illustrated/Getty Images; 15, © Nuccio DiNuzzo/Chicago Tribune/MCT/Landov; 16, © Doug Pensinger/Getty Images; 17, © Joe Robbins/Getty Images; 18, © David Eulitt/Kansas City Star/MCT/Landov; 19, © Doug Pensinger/Getty Images; 20, © Jeff Haynes/Reuters/Landov; 21, © AP Photo/Kevin Terrell; 22L, © AP Photo/David Stluka; 22R, © AP Photo/Matt Ludtke; 22Background, © AP Photo/Kevin Terrell.

Publisher: Kenn Goin
Senior Editor: Lisa Wiseman
Creative Director: Spencer Brinker
Design: Debrah Kaiser
Photo Researcher: Picture Perfect Professionals, LLC

Library of Congress Cataloging-in-Publication Data

Sandler, Michael, 1965–
  Aaron Rodgers and the Green Bay Packers: Super Bowl XLV / by Michael Sandler ; consultant, James Alder.
    p. cm. — (Super bowl superstars)
  Includes bibliographical references and index.
  ISBN-13: 978-1-61772-309-4 (library binding)
  ISBN-10: 1-61772-309-6 (library binding)
  1. Rodgers, Aaron, 1983—Juvenile literature. 2. Football players—United States—Biography—Juvenile literature. 3. Quarterbacks (Football) —United States—Biography—Juvenile literature. 4. Green Bay Packers (Football team) —Juvenile literature. 5. Super Bowl (45th : 2011 : Arlington, Tex.) I. Title. II. Series.

  GV939.R6235S26 2012
  796.332092—dc22
  (B)
                              2011013436

For more information, write to Bearport Publishing Company, Inc., 45 West 21st Street, Suite 3B, New York, New York 10010. Printed in the United States of America in North Mankato, Minnesota.

071511
042711CGD

10 9 8 7 6 5 4 3 2 1

☆ Contents ☆

Aaron's Test 4

Football Dreams 6

Dreams on Hold. 8

Breaking Out with the Bears 10

Filling In for Favre 12

Bringing the Cheers 14

The Big Game Begins 16

Pittsburgh Pushes Back. 18

Green Bay's Glory. 20

Key Players. 22

Glossary 23

Bibliography. 24

Read More. 24

Learn More Online 24

Index 24

Aaron's Test

Super Bowl XLV (45) was the final test for Aaron Rodgers. For six years, the Green Bay passer had been trying to win over the fans who doubted him. Now he had a chance to prove he was a great Packers quarterback. With a Super Bowl victory, no one would be able to doubt him any longer.

For this to happen, though, Aaron would have to beat a mighty **opponent**—the Pittsburgh Steelers. The Steelers had won six Super Bowls—an NFL record. They were a team that could score points easily, and their defense was fierce and effective. Running the ball against Pittsburgh's defenders was nearly impossible. For Green Bay to win, Aaron Rodgers would have to throw the ball perfectly.

Aaron Rodgers before the start of Super Bowl XLV (45) on February 6, 2011

Green Bay and Pittsburgh were both "super" Super Bowl teams. Before Super Bowl XLV (45), Pittsburgh had played in seven Super Bowls with six wins. Green Bay had played in four, winning three championships.

Football Dreams

For Aaron, being a Super Bowl quarterback was a lifelong dream. As a child growing up in Oregon and Northern California, he'd lived and breathed football. In kindergarten, he rounded up classmates for football games at recess, and always got to be the passer. Outside of school, he played football with his older brother, Luke, and his father, Ed.

Ed Rodgers didn't let his sons play organized football until high school. He worried about them getting hurt. So Aaron had to wait until he arrived at Pleasant Valley High School to truly show off his talents, of which he had many. Aaron could pass, he could run, and he knew how to lead a team.

Aaron also played baseball in high school.

Aaron tries to escape a tackle during a high school game.

Aaron passed for more than 4,400 yards (4,023 m) in two seasons at Pleasant Valley High School in Chico, California.

Dreams on Hold

Despite his success at Pleasant Valley High School, Aaron's football dreams nearly ended after high school. At just 175 pounds (79 kg) and barely six feet (1.83 m) tall, he was ignored by **recruiters** from the big football colleges. Many coaches and **scouts** thought he wasn't big enough to be a great college quarterback. Others worried that he wasn't athletic enough, or didn't have a strong throwing arm.

Frustrated, Aaron thought about quitting football. Instead, he decided to go to Butte College, a **community college**. Butte wasn't a **division I** football school, but the coach there offered Aaron a chance to play.

Aaron gets ready to take the field in a game for Butte.

Aaron said that Butte is "where I got my confidence. I never lost it."

Aaron had great success in one season at Butte. He threw 28 touchdowns and just 4 **interceptions**. His team had a 10–1 record and became one of the **highest-ranked** teams in the country.

Breaking Out with the Bears

Aaron's success at the small football school didn't go unnoticed. He caught the attention of Jeff Tedford, head coach at the University of California at Berkeley, a school with a strong football program. Coach Tedford drove up to Butte to watch Aaron practice. What he saw left him wowed. "I saw the talent... and he seemed to be a great leader on the field. I was sold," said Coach Tedford.

While driving back to Berkeley, he called Aaron and offered him a **scholarship**. Aaron's football dreams were alive again!

For two years, Aaron played quarterback for the university's Golden Bears football team. He threw for thousands of yards, and became known as a quarterback who rarely threw an interception.

Aaron (#8) scrambles down the field while playing for the Golden Bears.

After two years with the Golden Bears, Aaron entered the NFL **draft** in 2005. The Green Bay Packers chose him in the first round.

Aaron with his family on draft day in 2005

Aaron wasn't joining just any NFL team. The Packers were special. Their glorious history included wins in the first two Super Bowls ever played in 1967 and 1968. They also had superstar quarterback Brett Favre, who had led Green Bay to a third Super Bowl title in 1997.

For three years, Aaron waited patiently as Brett's **backup**. Then, in 2008, when Brett left to play for the New York Jets, Aaron finally got a chance to start.

Stepping into Brett Favre's shoes wasn't easy. Green Bay fans expected wins from their quarterback and their team. When the Packers went just 6–10 in Aaron's first season, he often heard boos from the stands.

Brett Favre

Green Bay is one of the winningest teams in NFL history. When Aaron joined the team, the Packers already had 12 titles, including victories in Super Bowl I (1), Super Bowl II (2), and Super Bowl XXXI (31).

Bringing the Cheers

Soon Aaron was turning those boos into cheers. During his second season as the starter, in 2009–2010, Aaron led Green Bay into the playoffs with an 11–5 record. He impressed fans with his quick release, **scrambling** skills, and on-field leadership.

His third season was even better. Despite injuries to many Green Bay players, Aaron led the Packers back into the playoffs. During games against the Philadelphia Eagles, the Atlanta Falcons, and the Chicago Bears, he played superbly and guided Green Bay into Super Bowl XLV (45). If Green Bay fans still doubted Aaron, he could change their minds with a Super Bowl win.

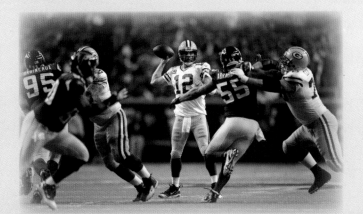

Aaron threw for 366 yards (335 m) and three touchdowns in the playoff game against the Falcons.

Aaron (#12) didn't just make great passes in the win against the Bears. He also made a touchdown-saving tackle on Chicago defender Brian Urlacher (#54).

Aaron Rodgers is the first quarterback in NFL history to throw ten touchdowns in his first three playoff games.

The Big Game Begins

Both Aaron and his team looked sharp when Super Bowl XLV (45), against the Pittsburgh Steelers, began on February 6, 2011. Just 12 minutes into the first quarter, Aaron lofted a 29-yard (27-m) touchdown pass to **wide receiver** Jordy Nelson. Green Bay had a quick 7–0 lead.

When the Steelers got the ball back, Green Bay **safety** Nick Collins **picked off** Pittsburgh quarterback Ben Roethlisberger. Nick ran the ball back 37 yards (34 m) into the **end zone**, giving the Packers a 14–0 lead.

Not even a Steelers field goal could discourage them. Aaron continued his great play and threw a 21-yard (19-m) touchdown pass to wide receiver Greg Jennings. Now the Packers were leading, 21–3.

Jordy Nelson (#87) catches a 29-yard (27-m) pass from Aaron to score a touchdown.

Greg Jennings (#85) leaps up to grab a 21-yard (19-m) touchdown pass from Aaron.

Greg Jennings's touchdown gave Green Bay an 18-point lead over Pittsburgh. No team in Super Bowl history had ever come back to win after falling so far behind.

Pittsburgh Pushes Back

Pittsburgh, however, wasn't giving up—no matter what the score was. Just before halftime, Ben Roethlisberger hit receiver Hines Ward for a touchdown, tightening the score to 21–10. When the second half started, the Steelers played defense with a new **intensity**. Suddenly, Aaron and the Packers found it impossible to gain yards.

Pittsburgh gained plenty of them, however. They **dominated** Green Bay with their **ground game**. When Steelers running back Rashard Mendenhall scored on an 8-yard (7-m) run, the Packers' lead shrank to just four points, 21–17. Was Pittsburgh about to complete the greatest comeback in Super Bowl history?

Aaron (#12) gets tackled by Pittsburgh Steelers linebacker James Harrison (#92).

Pittsburgh Steelers Hines Ward (#86) catches a touchdown pass.

Injuries were also making things tough for Green Bay. Their best defender, **cornerback** Charles Woodson, was knocked out of the game just before halftime when he suffered a broken collarbone.

The Packers didn't let it happen. On the final quarter's first play, Green Bay linebacker Clay Matthews smashed into Rashard Mendenhall, forcing a **fumble**. The Packers took **possession**, and Aaron passed to Greg Jennings for a touchdown and a 28–17 lead.

Then, after another Ben Roethlisberger touchdown pass had closed the gap to 28–25, Aaron responded again. He slowly brought Green Bay downfield, eating five minutes off the clock. The **drive** finished with a field goal that gave the Packers a 31–25 lead.

Two minutes later, the final whistle blew. Green Bay had won Super Bowl XLV (45). Aaron Rodgers was a Super Bowl-winning quarterback! No one could doubt him any longer.

Green Bay Packers Clay Matthews (#52) knocks the ball out of Steelers running back Rashard Mendenhall's (#34) hands.

Aaron holds the Super Bowl trophy.

Aaron was named Super Bowl MVP for his performance. He threw 24 **completions** in 39 attempts for 304 passing yards (278 m), and 3 touchdowns.

There were other key players on the Green Bay Packers who helped win Super Bowl XLV (45). Here are two of them.

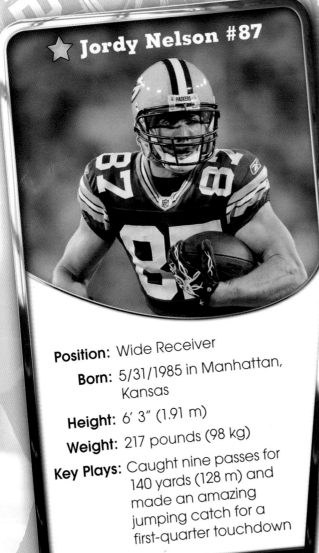

★ **Jordy Nelson #87**

Position: Wide Receiver

Born: 5/31/1985 in Manhattan, Kansas

Height: 6′ 3″ (1.91 m)

Weight: 217 pounds (98 kg)

Key Plays: Caught nine passes for 140 yards (128 m) and made an amazing jumping catch for a first-quarter touchdown

★ **Greg Jennings #85**

Position: Wide Receiver

Born: 9/21/1983 in Kalamazoo, Michigan

Height: 5′ 11″ (1.80 m)

Weight: 198 pounds (90 kg)

Key Plays: Caught two touchdown passes, including the key fourth-quarter Green Bay touchdown

backup (BAK-uhp) a player who doesn't play at the start of a game; the second-best player at a position

community college (kuh-MYOO-nuh-tee KOL-ij) a college that offers a two-year course of study, rather than four years

completions (kuhm-PLEE-shuhnz) passes thrown by the quarterback that are caught by receivers

cornerback (KOR-nur-bak) a defensive player who has the job of covering the other team's receivers

division I (di-VIZH-uhn WON) the group of schools that compete at the highest level of college sports

dominated (DOM-uh-*nay*-tid) completely outplayed

draft (DRAFT) an event in which pro teams take turns choosing college players to play for them

drive (DRIVE) a series of plays that begin when a team gets the ball; the plays end when the team with the ball either scores or gives up the ball to the other team

end zone (END ZOHN) areas at either end of a football field where touchdowns are scored

fumble (FUHM-buhl) a ball that is dropped or lost by the player who has it

ground game (GROUND GAME) plays that involve running the ball rather than passing the ball

highest-ranked (HYE-est-RANGKT) believed to be the best

intensity (in-TEN-suh-tee) a high level of action and effort

interceptions (*in*-tur-SEP-shuhnz) passes caught by defensive players on the other team, rather than the offensive players they were intended for

opponent (uh-POH-nuhnt) a team that another team plays against

picked off (PIKT AWF) intercepted; catching a pass meant for a receiver on the other team

possession (puh-ZESH-uhn) when a team has the ball and is trying to score

recruiters (ri-KROOT-urz) people whose job it is to convince talented players to come and play for a college's sports teams

safety (SAYF-tee) a defensive player who lines up farther back than other defensive players

scholarship (SKOL-ur-ship) an award that helps pay for a person to go to college

scouts (SKOUTS) people who search for talented players to play on professional teams

scrambling (SKRAM-buhl-ing) the ability to run away from defenders to avoid being tackled

wide receiver (WIDE ri-SEE-vur) a player whose job it is to catch passes

Bibliography

Hack, Damon. "Mr. Rodgers' Neighborhood." *Sports Illustrated* (October 11, 2010).

Kroichick, Ron. "Profile: Aaron Rodgers, Cal Quarterback." *San Francisco Chronicle* (December 26, 2004).

Tedford, Jeff, and Steve Greenberg. "You Don't Know Aaron Rodgers Like I Know Aaron Rodgers." *Sporting News* (August 30, 2010).

NFL.com

Read More

MacRae, Sloan. *The Green Bay Packers (America's Greatest Teams).* New York: PowerKids Press (2011).

Sandler, Michael. *Pro Football's Most Spectacular Quarterbacks (Football-O-Rama).* New York: Bearport (2011).

Sandler, Michael. *Santonio Holmes and the Pittsburgh Steelers: Super Bowl XLIII (Super Bowl Superstars).* New York: Bearport (2010).

Learn More Online

To learn more about Aaron Rodgers,
the Green Bay Packers, and the Super Bowl, visit
www.bearportpublishing.com/SuperBowlSuperstars

Index

Atlanta Falcons 14

Butte College 8–9, 10

Chicago Bears 14–15

Chico, California 7

Collins, Nick 16

Favre, Brett 12

Jennings, Greg 16–17, 20, 22

Matthews, Clay 20

Mendenhall, Rashard 18, 20

Nelson, Jordy 16, 22

Philadelphia Eagles 14

Pittsburgh Steelers 4–5, 16–17, 18–19, 20

Pleasant Valley High School 6–7, 8

Rodgers, Ed 6

Rodgers, Luke 6

Roethlisberger, Ben 16, 18, 20

Tedford, Jeff 10

University of California at Berkeley 10–11

Ward, Hines 18–19

Woodson, Charles 19